THE LAST ADAM
THE STANDARD FOR WHAT'S AVAILABLE IN CHRIST

CHAD GONZALES

CONTENTS

Introduction	v
1. You Are About To Live	1
2. Out With The Old	5
3. In With The New	11
4. Greater Works	17
5. A Heavenly Perspective	21
6. It's An Identity Thing	25
7. One With Christ	31
8. Enough Excuses	37
9. What's Possible	43
About the Author	49
Other Books Written By Chad	51
Prayer For Salvation And The Baptism Of The Holy Spirit	53
The Supernatural Life Podcast	57
The Healing Academy	59
More From CGM	61

Scripture quotations taken from the New King James Version. Copyright © 1982 by Thomas Nelson, Inc. Used by permission. All rights reserved.

Scripture quotations taken from the Amplified® Bible, Copyright © 1954, 1958, 1962, 1964, 1965, 1987 by The Lockman Foundation. Used by permission. (www.Lockman.org)

Scripture taken from The Message. Copyright 1993, 1994, 1995, 1996, 2000, 2001, 2002. Used by permission of NavPress Publishing Group.

Scripture taken from the HOLY BIBLE, NEW INTERNATIONAL VERSION®. Copyright © 1973, 1978, 1984 Biblica. Used by permission of Zondervan. All rights reserved.

Scripture quotations are taken from the Holy Bible, New Living Translation, copyright 1996, 2004. Used by permission of Tyndale House Publishers, Inc., Wheaton, Illinois 60189. All rights reserved.

The Last Adam

ISBN: 979-8-9916262-6-2

Copyright © 2025 by Chad W. Gonzales

Chad Gonzales Ministries

www.ChadGonzales.com

Printed in the United States of America. All rights reserved under International Copyright Law. Contents and/or cover may not be reproduced in whole or in part in any form without the express written consent of the Publisher or Author.

INTRODUCTION

When I look at Jesus and realize that He's the standard for what's available for every single one of us, you know what that does? Number one, it shoots holes in a lot of the doctrine that we've been told before. Number two, it makes you just want to go even further and inspires you to go further once you see what's actually possible.

I want you to see in Scripture and get a glimpse, for what's actually possible for you as a believer. It is amazing what it begins to do to you when you find out that we have sold ourselves short on our salvation and what that truly entails.

The vast majority of Christians think that salvation really is just about going to heaven. They think eternal life begins when I step out of this body instead of realizing that, the day I accepted Jesus as my Lord and Savior, my eternal life began and my life was supposed to look just like Him.

ONE
YOU ARE ABOUT TO LIVE

In John 14, the scene is in the upper room—right before Jesus goes to the garden of Gethsemane to turn Himself over. He's there with His disciples, and in verse 19 He makes a powerful statement:

John 14:19 NKJV

A little while longer and the world will see Me no more, but you will see Me. Because I live, you will live also.

Put yourself in the disciples' position and think about what was just said. Jesus is standing next to His friends, His partners, and then He tells them: *"In a couple of days, you're going to become alive."*

These are the kinds of statements Jesus makes that hardly anybody talks about—because they're radical, wild, and way beyond our natural thinking. They don't make sense to the mind. But imagine this: Jesus is sitting at the table with His friends during the Passover meal, looks across at them and says, *"Hey, I've got good news. You're about to become alive."*

Now, what would you do? You're sitting at the coffee shop with a buddy. You're thinking maybe they're going to buy you a donut, and instead they say, *"In three days, you're going to come alive!"* I don't know about you, but I'd wonder if they had a little something extra in their coffee!

Jesus isn't talking to someone in a casket here. He's talking to His disciples—physically alive, sitting at the table, about to take the Passover meal. And He tells them, *"In just a few days, you're going to live."*

What does that mean? What does that look like? *"You're going to become alive."*

Now, we've all heard the phrase "born again," right? But what does that really mean? A lot of people think it's like getting a golden Willy Wonka ticket to heaven, or that it means you'll become a better person—stop using as many bad words, give a little more money, cut down on bad habits. And then one day you'll get to heaven, walk through the pearly gates, give Peter a high five, and say, *"Thank God, I made it!"*

Why do people think that way? Because we've turned salvation into behavior modification.

But Jesus looks at His friends and says, *"In three days, you're going to become alive."* If I were sitting there, I'd be looking at my cup thinking, *"What's in this wine?"*

So what does it mean? What does that entail? What actually changes?

When I received Jesus as my Lord and Savior, nothing on the outside changed. I thought maybe I'd get taller—but that didn't happen! And when you look at the disciples, when they received Jesus as Lord and Savior, nothing visibly changed on the outside either. Why? Because being born again isn't about your body. You are not a body. You are a spirit.

This is what Jesus was talking about: *"You are going to become alive."* The disciples were physically alive, but spiritually dead. Jesus was telling them that in three days they would become spiritually alive.

So what does that really mean for us? Let's find out what actually happened to you the day you said, *"Jesus, be the Lord and Savior of my life."*

TWO
OUT WITH THE OLD

1 Corinthians 15:45 NKJV

So it is written: "The first man Adam became a living being. The last Adam became a life-giving spirit."

There are two things I want you to see here. First, Paul is telling us what Jesus came to do: Jesus was a life-giver. He came to give you life, but not physical life, spiritual life.

Second, notice Jesus is referred to as "the last Adam." So what does "last" mean? You don't need a degree to figure that out; a first grader can. If I had a bag of Reese's Pieces and gave you the last one, what does that mean? It means there are no more left!

Jesus came as the last Adam—the final one. He came to finish off the Adamic race and to start something brand new. That's right! Jesus came to start something brand new.

This is where 2 Corinthians 5:17 becomes a greater reality for us:

2 Corinthians 5:17 NKJV

Therefore, if anyone is in Christ, he is a new creation; old things have passed away; behold, all things have become new.

2 Corinthians 5:17 TPT

Now, if anyone is enfolded into Christ, he has become an entirely new person. All that is related to the old order has vanished. Behold, everything is fresh and new.

What does "new" mean? It means something that didn't exist before. When you get saved, you are placed in Christ and become a new creation.

Old things have passed away. All things have become new. What does "all" mean? "All" means the entire quantity, the whole of something.

Look at these words: *Last. New. All.* None of these are complicated, but we've overcomplicated salvation because it doesn't fit in our small view of what it really is.

Jesus was the last Adam, and He came to begin a new

creation so the old way of living could be gone forever. Some translations put it this way: *"The old life has gone, and a new life has begun."*

Now, here's the religious view: "Oh yeah, so now you don't cuss anymore. You don't smoke anymore. You don't drink. You don't sleep around. You don't do those things anymore. You're just going to be a better person."

Friend, that's not what Jesus taught. Jesus didn't come to make you a better moral person. I know people of other religions who have higher morals than some Christians I know. I've got friends from certain denominations who will party on Saturday night and then go to Mass the next day.

Listen, Jesus didn't come to just change your behavior. He came to make you into something that never existed before: a new creation in Christ.

So where is this new creation found? It starts **in Him.** When you're born again, you receive a brand-new identity. The old life is gone, and a new life has begun.

But hear me on this. It's not just about behavior. Yes, as believers we should grow, change, and live with higher standards. But you don't have to be saved to clean up your morals. Plenty of people do that without Jesus.

So what is this new life all about? You have to look at Jesus.

The new life starts in Him, because Jesus is the life-giving Spirit. I have to look at Him to know what this new life looks like.

Romans 6:4 NKJV

Therefore we were buried with Him through baptism into death, that just as Christ was raised from the dead by the glory of the Father, even so we also should walk in newness of life.

We were buried with Him. That means when Jesus died, in the eyes of God, I died. The old Chad is gone!

What's the result? On the spiritual side, I identify with His death. So to understand what I died to, I have to look at what Jesus died to.

Isaiah 53:4–5 AMPC

Surely He has borne our griefs (sicknesses, weaknesses, and distresses) and carried our sorrows and pains [of punishment], yet we [ignorantly] considered Him stricken, smitten, and afflicted by God [as if with leprosy]. But He was wounded for our transgressions, He was bruised for our guilt and iniquities; the chastisement [needful to obtain] peace and well-being for us was upon Him, and with the stripes [that wounded] Him we are healed and made whole.

When I died with Jesus, He not only became my sin—He also became my disease.

2 Corinthians 5:21 says Jesus became sin so we could become the righteousness of God in Christ. So the first part of identifying with Jesus' death is understanding what I died with.

If Jesus died with sin and sickness, then I died with them too. That stuff is dead to me now!

THREE
IN WITH THE NEW

Romans 6:4 AMPC

We were buried therefore with Him by the baptism into death, so that just as Christ was raised from the dead by the glorious [power] of the Father, so we too might [habitually] live and behave in newness of life.

Notice what Paul says here: *"just as Christ."* That's not a complicated phrase, but we tend to get religious with it and make it complicated. What does "just as" mean? It means *in the very same way.*

In the very same way Jesus is experiencing a new life, I'm supposed to experience a new life. *Just as… even so.* Simple words with a massive implication.

So what is my new life supposed to look like? I have to

look at Jesus' current life to know what my life on earth should look like.

Now, this raises a problem for most of us: Jesus is in heaven, and we're on the earth. Where's Jesus physically? At the right hand of God.

Colossians 3:1–3 AMPC

If then you have been raised with Christ [to a new life, thus sharing His resurrection from the dead], aim at and seek the [rich, eternal treasures] that are above, where Christ is, seated at the right hand of God. And set your minds and keep them set on what is above (the higher things), not on the things that are on the earth. For [as far as this world is concerned] you have died, and your [new, real] life is hidden with Christ in God.

Colossians 3:1–3 TPT

Christ's resurrection is your resurrection too. This is why we are to yearn for all that is above, for that's where Christ sits enthroned at the place of all power, honor, and authority! Yes, feast on all the treasures of the heavenly realm and fill your thoughts with heavenly realities, and not with the distractions of the natural realm. Your crucifixion with Christ has severed the tie to this life, and now your true life is hidden away in God in Christ.

We died with Christ, we were raised with Christ, and now our new life is hidden with Christ. Do you see the massive realities here?

Colossians 3:10 NKJV

And have put on the new man who is renewed in knowledge according to the image of Him who created him.

Colossians 3:10 TPT

For you have acquired new creation life which is continually being renewed into the likeness of the One who created you; giving you the full revelation of God.

Paul tells us in verse 10 that we must renew our minds according to the One who created us. That means we have to look at Jesus to understand who we are, what we have, and what we can do. We are the image of Jesus! When you see Him, you should see yourself.

Religious people have a problem with this, because Satan doesn't want you to know who you really are. Remember what Jesus said in John 14: *"If you've seen Me, you've seen the Father."* Most people don't argue with that —until you point out that Jesus said this as a man.

The moment you see Jesus speaking and doing miracles as a man filled with God, it changes everything. It moves you from just admiring Him to identifying with

Him. It shifts you from standing back and only worshiping, to standing in His shoes and doing.

Philippians 2:5–8 NKJV

Let this mind be in you which was also in Christ Jesus, who, being in the form of God, did not consider it robbery to be equal with God, but made Himself of no reputation, taking the form of a bondservant, and coming in the likeness of men. And being found in appearance as a man, He humbled Himself and became obedient to the point of death, even the death of the cross.

We must understand this: Jesus did life as a man. Yet He told His disciples, *"If you've seen Me on earth, you've seen My Father in heaven."*

Think about that!

Jesus wasn't only showing what was possible for a man filled with God, united with God, anointed by God. He was showing that your location doesn't determine your identity. If you want to know what God is like, look at Jesus. But if you want to know what you're like, look at Jesus.

Here's where it all comes together: Jesus reveals that as a spirit being, it's possible to live as a man on earth while being like God in heaven.

1 John 4:17 NKJV

Love has been perfected among us in this: that we may have boldness in the day of judgment; because as He is, so are we in this world.

If you want to know what you can truly do and have on this planet, you need to look at Jesus right now. *As He is, so are we in this world.* That's present tense.

Where is Jesus? Physically in heaven. Which means the way Jesus is in heaven is the way I am on earth.

Most Christians never get this far. They'd rather just talk about not sinning anymore. And yes, of course we shouldn't be living in sin—but let's be honest, if you've been struggling with the same sin for 20 or 30 years, you need to get born again.

Sin is baby stuff. We've got to move beyond behavior modification and start teaching identification. We need to renew our minds and see ourselves the way heaven sees us.

The moment you start to understand who you are, you'll start acting like it.

Think about when you put on a costume. (I know, you don't celebrate Halloween—it's "Hallelujah Night" for us church folks.) But even then, when you put on a costume, you instinctively start acting like that character. Even if you're usually reserved, you slip into the persona.

In the same way, when you receive Jesus, you didn't just put on something new—you became something new. A brand-new creation.

And because you're a new creation, you can't even look at Old Testament people as your example of how to live. Why? Every single one of them was still a sinner.

FOUR
GREATER WORKS

We need to understand this: Jesus, even though He was the righteousness of God in Christ, was still operating under the Old Covenant. When Jesus prays in John 17, He reveals a tremendous reality with powerful implications for us as new creations.

John 17:5 TPT

"So my Father, restore me back to the glory that we shared together when we were face-to-face before the universe was created."

That right there tells you Jesus wasn't even walking in all the glory that was available. But wait—it gets even better.

The day Jesus rose from the dead, He stood before the disciples—the future Church—and declared:

Matthew 28:18–20 NKJV

And Jesus came and spoke to them, saying, "All authority has been given to Me in heaven and on earth. Go therefore and make disciples of all the nations, baptizing them in the name of the Father and of the Son and of the Holy Spirit, teaching them to observe all things that I have commanded you; and lo, I am with you always, even to the end of the age." Amen.

When Jesus sent out the twelve in Luke 9 and the seventy in Luke 10, He said, *"I give you authority over all sickness and all disease."* But the day He stripped Satan of authority and rose victorious, Jesus stood as the firstborn from the dead and said, *"Now all of it is Mine."*

Jesus came as the last Adam to be the first of a new creation. That's why He said in John 14:12: *"Whoever believes in Me will not only do the same works (according to the last Adam) but will also do greater works (according to the glorified Christ)."*

How was that going to happen? Salvation. *"Whoever believes in Me will not only do the same…"* Think about it. When He sent out the twelve and the seventy, they were doing the same works He was doing.

And before anyone gets religious and says, "Well, the only reason Jesus was performing miracles was because He was the Son of God," let's use some common sense.

What about the guys in the Old Testament? Moses parted the Red Sea. Moses—a former murderer and still a sinner—did miracle after miracle. One of the most astounding was when, even in disobedience, he struck a rock and caused a river to flow for millions of people and animals.

Jesus wasn't the first to multiply food either. Elijah did it for 100 people. So where's your excuse?

Jesus wasn't the first to raise someone from the dead. Remember, Jesus grew up as a Jewish boy. He had to read the Law and the Prophets. He read about Moses, Elijah, Elisha. He was inspired by what was possible under the Old Covenant—and yet He came to show us what was possible for a righteous man, unified with God, filled with God… even under the limitations of the Old Covenant.

And Jesus said, *"You'll do that. But because I'm going to the Father—because salvation is coming—you'll do even more."*

In other words: *Guys, look at what you've been doing while spiritually dead. In three days, you're going to become spiritually alive. And what you've been doing up until now will be the floor of what's available for the Church.*

See, here's the problem: the religious, small-minded, no-backbone church of today looks at the works of Jesus as the ceiling. But Jesus came to make those works the floor.

So how can we do greater works if we keep seeing Jesus' works as the greatest? We've got to flip it. We need to look at what Jesus did and say, *"That's minimal. That's the starting point."*

And no—that's not blasphemy. That's the reality of being a new creation in Christ.

FIVE
A HEAVENLY PERSPECTIVE

Colossians 3:1–3 NLT

Since you have been raised to new life with Christ, set your sights on the realities of heaven, where Christ sits in the place of honor at God's right hand. Think about the things of heaven, not the things of earth. For you died to this life, and your real life is hidden with Christ in God.

I must begin renewing my mind to the possibilities of the glorified Christ.

You died, and now there is a new you—a new creation in Christ. That's why Paul says to set your mind on the realities of heaven. Why? Because you need to see what's available. But it's more than simply setting your mind on heaven in general. It's setting your mind on what's available at the throne.

Ephesians 2 tells us that we were raised up and seated at the right hand of God. That throne room is the place you pray from, minister from, worship from, and live from. Why do you think you can boldly go before the throne of grace to find help in time of need? Because that's where He positioned you!

Most Christians think that when they get to heaven, they'll walk into the throne room, fall to their knees, and beg: *"I'm unworthy, I'm unworthy, I'm unworthy."* No, friend. When you understand you are the righteousness of God in Christ, you'll walk boldly into that place—not out of disrespect, but because you know who you are.

My son Jake has never come up to me and said, *"Dad, I know I'm not good enough, but can I please have something from the fridge?"* No, he just boldly walks into the pantry. And if there's something we don't have, he simply asks, *"Dad, when are we going to the store?"* That's what righteousness looks like in action—confidence in relationship.

I believe one reason the Bible emphasizes that God seated us with Him is because so many Christians still sit back and think, *"I'm not good enough."* The Gospel is astounding—and yet it's so simple. That's why it's a stumbling block to so many people. It feels too good to be true!

We look at Jesus and at the Old Testament prophets and are amazed at what they did. But when you step back and see from the perspective of the new creation, you realize: we actually have it better.

One of our biggest problems is that we still look at life through the lens of a sinner instead of the lens of a new creation. We're trying to see heavenly realities through earthly eyes. That's why we've sold ourselves short and why we don't see the miracles we should be seeing.

So why do people still question God's will concerning healing? Why do people still think He's holding out on them? Because they're trying to understand new creation realities with an old creation mindset—saying, *"I'm saved,"* but still living like a sinner.

Jesus was trying to get this across: *"Everything you've seen Me do—that's the minimum compared to what's coming in three days. You're going to become alive. You're going to become a new creation. The old way of living is gone. All the limitations are gone. Something brand new is starting."*

We need to realize that Jesus came to create something entirely new. In John 17, He prayed: *"Father, the glory You gave Me, I have given to them."*

The disciples operated with the same Spirit Jesus carried while He walked the earth. But when they were born again, everything shifted to another level. That's why they began to do greater works.

This is what you see in Acts. Peter's shadow falling on people and healings breaking out. People bringing cloths from Paul's body to the sick and demon-possessed, and those people being set free. Why? Because the life of God was so strong in him that it flowed from his spirit into his skin, into his clothes, into those cloths.

James 5 takes the same approach. James instructs believers: if there's someone in such dire condition they can't believe for themselves, simply pray the prayer of faith, lay hands on them, and the Lord will raise them up. That was supposed to be normal practice for abnormal circumstances.

And James, one of the main leaders of the early church, adds: if sin was involved, God will forgive that too.

Yet look at how the modern church treats this passage. We've made laying on of hands into something mechanical, something we "try." James wasn't giving us a ritual to test out—he was describing how a healed, untouchable Church should respond if someone happens to stumble.

Sickness isn't supposed to be normal in the Church; healing is.

SIX
IT'S AN IDENTITY THING

Friend, this new creation reality is simple: if you want to know what's possible and what's normal, you have to look at the way Jesus is *right now*.

So why would we make "normal" for the new creation the same as what's normal for the sinner? Let's be honest: what's considered normal in the world has, in many ways, become normal in the Church.

Even in the area of healing, let me ask you: shouldn't the person filled with the devil have different results than the person filled with God?

Is Jesus getting sick? Then why are we? Do you know why? Because we think it's normal. We've allowed what's normal for the sinner to become normal for the new creation.

The real issue is this: we've been interpreting the Bible wrong. I've taught this for years and gotten flack for it—but I don't really care at this point.

Think about it. Every person Jesus ministered to before the cross was spiritually dead. Everyone outside of Him was a sinner. Every blind man, every deaf person, every leper—all sinners. Every single person Jesus healed, every person He raised from the dead, was spiritually dead.

Yet how do most people teach healing? They tell you to go look at the sinner to figure out how to get healed. I used to do the same thing because it's what I was taught. But look at the Gospels. Out of the 19 individual healings recorded, show me one righteous person. Show me one who was born again. Show me one who was filled with the Spirit or one with God. You won't find one.

- They were all spiritually dead.

- None of them had the life of God inside.

- None were temples of the Holy Spirit.

- None were righteous.

- None were redeemed by the blood of the Lamb.

They had to go to someone who was carrying God.

Yet today, teachers will still say, "By the stripes of Jesus, you were healed," and then point you to the woman with the issue of blood to figure out how to receive healing. Or they'll point you to the centurion's servant, or to Jairus, or some other sinner's story as your example. But why would I, as one with Christ, have to receive healing like a sinner who was separate from God?

We've created an identity crisis in the Church. While the world can't even figure out male from female, the Church can't seem to figure out whether we're sinners or saints.

What would happen if we stopped identifying with the woman with the issue of blood and started identifying with Jesus? What would happen if we stopped identifying as those in need of healing and started identifying as those who carry healing?

It's an identity issue! The reason many believers still struggle is because their perspective on what actually happened at the new birth is wrong. We've been focused on possessions—what we can get—instead of identification, who we already are.

1 Peter 2:24 is a perfect example. Ask most Christians what it says, and they'll answer, *"By His stripes we were healed."* But that's not the whole verse, and it's not just about healing—it's about identity.

1 Peter 2:24 NKJV

Who Himself bore our sins in His own body on the tree, that we, having died to sins, might live for righteousness—by whose stripes you were healed.

Peter isn't telling you what to go get; he's telling you who you are. You became righteous. You became perfect. You became complete. Healing flows out of that righteousness.

And for those who argue Peter wasn't talking about physical healing—then why did Matthew apply the very same prophecy to Jesus physically healing people?

Matthew 8:16–17 TPT

That evening the people brought to Him many who were demonized. And by Jesus only speaking a word of healing over them, they were totally set free from their torment, and everyone who was sick received their healing! In doing this, Jesus fulfilled the prophecy of Isaiah: He put upon Himself our weaknesses, and He carried away our diseases and made us well.

Isaiah was talking about physical sickness. Matthew applied it to physical sickness. Peter was quoting Isaiah.

You died to sin and sickness. A new life has begun.

So why is sickness still normal for so many Christians?

Because we've been told it is. Sickness is the byproduct of unrighteousness, just as healing is the byproduct of righteousness. Sickness is normal for the sinner—but why should it be normal for the new creation?

During COVID, everyone kept talking about a "new normal." But the world's normal is still sickness. Friend, there's no new normal in the curse.

At some point, you've got to rise up and say, *"Enough is enough!"* This new creation life isn't supposed to look like the world. It's not even supposed to look like Jesus during His earthly ministry—it's supposed to look like Jesus glorified.

That's the new creation reality: a life united with Him.

SEVEN
ONE WITH CHRIST

In John chapters 13–17, we find Jesus in the upper room with His disciples. He's spending His last hours with them before He turns Himself over to the soldiers in the garden of Gethsemane. Before they leave, Jesus prays a supernatural, prophetic prayer in John 17.

In my opinion, if there ever was a "Lord's Prayer," it's John 17. (For an in-depth study, see my book *The Supernatural Prayer of Jesus*.)

In this prayer, Jesus not only prays for Himself and the disciples with Him—He also begins to pray out the plan of God for the new creation, which includes us!

John 17:20–23 NKJV

"I do not pray for these alone, but also for those who will believe in Me through their word; that they all may

be one, as You, Father, are in Me, and I in You; that they also may be one in Us, that the world may believe that You sent Me. And the glory which You gave Me I have given them, that they may be one just as We are one: I in them, and You in Me; that they may be made perfect in one, and that the world may know that You have sent Me, and have loved them as You have loved Me."

Jesus prayed, *"Father, I pray that they would be one in Us so the world would know You sent Me."* How is the world supposed to know that God sent Jesus by looking at you and me? It's simple: we're supposed to look just like Him.

Our results should look like Him. Our words should sound like Him. Our actions should mirror His.

But here's the problem: when most churches talk about the Great Commission, they reduce it to something we can do without God—read a tract, hand out information, and try to convince someone to accept Jesus.

Isn't it interesting that Jesus actually believed the sinner would need to *see* something in order to believe the message? He listed signs like casting out devils, speaking in new tongues, immunity to deadly things, and laying hands on the sick so they would recover. Jesus believed that signs, wonders, and miracles would prove this almost-too-good-to-be-true news!

Yet what have we done? Even among the people who believe in signs and wonders, we've relegated them to "believer's meetings." And usually, we only have those as special events—because we don't want to offend first-time visitors on Sunday mornings!

So the very things Jesus gave us to reach the lost, we've tucked away for insider meetings with the saved. We've decided our way of reaching people is smarter than His way.

And what's the result? We've let the world's "normal" become our normal. Instead of healing the lost, most of us are still trying to get healed ourselves.

If you really want to get scriptural, consider this: in the book of Acts, there are only two times believers laid hands on other believers. And in both cases, the believers were dead!

The first was Eutychus. Paul was preaching long, the guy fell out of a window and died.

> **Acts 20:9–10 NKJV**
>
> *And in a window sat a certain young man named Eutychus, who was sinking into a deep sleep. He was overcome by sleep; and as Paul continued speaking, he fell down from the third story and was taken up dead. But Paul went down, fell on him, and embracing him said, "Do not trouble*

yourselves, for his life is in him."

Paul raised him up and then went right back to preaching until morning—probably finishing with breakfast!

The next believer was Tabitha (Dorcas).

Acts 9:36–40 NKJV

At Joppa there was a certain disciple named Tabitha, which is translated Dorcas. This woman was full of good works and charitable deeds which she did. But it happened in those days that she became sick and died. ... But Peter put them all out, and knelt down and prayed. And turning to the body he said, "Tabitha, arise." And she opened her eyes, and when she saw Peter she sat up.

So in all of Acts, we see two believers who had hands laid on them for a miracle—and both of them were dead.

The truth is, laying on of hands was supposed to be a tool for reaching sinners. But we've normalized it for the Church.

Now, I'm not saying it's wrong to lay hands on believers. Thank God we have every tool available to us. What I'm saying is, we've minimized salvation. We weren't meant to be dependent on another person to receive what Jesus already gave us. If you don't know who you are, you'll always chase something you already have.

Jesus came to unite you with God. The crowning achievement of His ministry was the union of man and God once again. That's why Paul writes:

1 Corinthians 6:17 NKJV

But he who is joined to the Lord is one spirit with Him.

And in Ephesians 5, Paul ties this union to marriage:

Ephesians 5:30–32 NKJV

For we are members of His body, of His flesh and of His bones. "For this reason a man shall leave his father and mother and be joined to his wife, and the two shall become one flesh." This is a great mystery, but I speak concerning Christ and the church.

At weddings we hear, *"bone of his bone, flesh of his flesh."* But Paul says this is actually about Christ and the Church.

Jesus is the husband, and we are the bride. As the bride, we take on His identity. When you were born again, you entered into covenant and took on His name.

That's why Paul could write in Ephesians 1:23 that we are *"the fullness of Him who fills all in all."*

It's why John could say, *"Of His fullness we have all received, and grace for grace."*

It's why Colossians 2:6 says, *"As you therefore have received Christ Jesus the Lord, so walk in Him."*

And it's why Colossians 2:9–10 says: *"For in Him dwells all the fullness of the Godhead bodily; and you are complete in Him."*

If you want to know who you are and what's possible as a new creation in Christ, you don't look at some man or woman who walked this earth. Thank God for their example, but they're not your standard.

Your standard is the glorified Christ, seated at the right hand of God.

And yes—when you start talking like this, people get upset. They'll say, *"Who do you think you are to believe you could do greater things than Jesus?"*

But here's the reality: if you don't believe greater is possible, you must believe Jesus is dead. Because if He's alive, He can certainly outdo Himself!

Jesus put us in position to be His body. He's the head, and we are the body. That means He can use our hands, our feet, our voices, and our lives. He's the vine, we're the branches, and everything that flows in Him flows in us.

EIGHT
ENOUGH EXCUSES

Instead of realizing who we are as the Church, we've gotten religious. We focus on titles and giftings—"We need this gift of the Spirit or that anointing to see miracles."

No. All you have to do is look at Jesus.

When He sent out the twelve and the seventy, He didn't say, *"Peter, I'm giving you an anointing for cancer. John, yours is for joints. James, yours is for ears."* No! The Church made that up. Jesus didn't.

Friend, people are like water—we always look for the path of least resistance. And most ministers today are operating in the natural, intellectual realm, searching for a verse to excuse their cowardice.

I once heard a respected minister say, *"Well, I'm a teacher. I just teach the Word. I don't need manifestations."* If I could, that's where I'd insert an eye-roll emoji.

Let's be honest. Even in Jesus' day, it was only 8% who had the guts to step out. Twelve disciples, and only one walked on water. Do the math: 8%.

Look at the parable of the sower. Four groups. Only one bore fruit—25%. And within that 25%, some bore 30, some 60, some 100-fold. Do the math again: the hundredfold crowd was only about 8%. In other words, since Jesus' day, only a small fraction have been bold enough to step out and go after everything available.

And honestly, nothing's gotten better. In fact, I'd say it's worse. If you think hundreds of millions are going to dive into this next great move of God—you're mistaken. Every revival in history was sparked by small groups. Even the Azusa Street revival (1906–1910) only had about 100 people in the room each night.

The thing we've been waiting on, fasting for, begging God for? If we'd simply recognize who we are, we'd start experiencing it.

Go back and read the stories of Jesus. Stop identifying with the sick, the desperate, the crowd pressing in. Start identifying with Christ—the one they were pressing in to touch. Identify with Christ, the one who walked in all authority, in whom power flowed so freely that just touching Him brought healing.

What if you began to think of yourself like that? Talk about a confidence boost. Those little nagging things that hound you would start to fall aside as you recognize who you are.

The Church doesn't know who it is. That's why so many believers are still afraid of Satan—afraid of the very things they've already been delivered from. That's why Christians are still struggling with the same junk the world struggles with.

Let me be blunt. When you got born again, what Jesus did was enough.

Right now, one of the most ridiculous teachings spreading in churches is about "redeeming your bloodline" to break generational curses. Friend, that's one of the dumbest things being peddled today. You cannot preach new creation realities and generational curses at the same time.

How can God be your Father and you still be cursed by your natural bloodline? He's the first generation, and you're the second. His past became your past. His bloodline became your bloodline. The bloodline flows from the Father—and if God is your Father, you're in His bloodline.

So why would you need to "redeem your bloodline" when you've already been redeemed by the Blood of the Lamb?

The only way you'd need to redeem it is if the devil is your daddy. And if that's the case, the solution is simple: get born again. And hey—it'll also save you $19.99 on some book teaching you how to fix what Jesus already did.

We keep looking for detours and excuses because the Gospel is so simple it offends our intellect. We'd rather complicate it and blame God for why things aren't working than actually renew our minds to who we are in Him.

How do you discover who you are? Look at Him. Over and over—look at Him.

Wouldn't it be amazing if the world could look at us and say, *"That's what Jesus looks like. That's what's possible."* Not because we say it, but because we live it.

When John the Baptist declared, *"This is the Christ!"* how did Jesus validate it? He didn't say, *"Look at my followers, my book sales, my TV network, my millions of subscribers."* He didn't point to His giving record.

Jesus based success on the supernatural.

John 10:37–38 NKJV

> *"If I do not do the works of My Father, do not believe Me; but if I do, though you do not believe Me, believe the works, that you may know and believe that the Father is in Me, and I in Him."*

Where are the preachers today who will lay it all on the line like that?

I'll never forget a deaf woman I met outside Walmart in Bryan, Texas. She was selling pencils and notepads. I asked if she believed in Jesus. She wrote "Yes." I asked if anyone had ever prayed for her hearing. She wrote, "Many times. Nothing happened."

She wasn't open, so I wrote on the pad: *"If you come to church this Sunday, I guarantee God will heal you. If not, I'll give you $100."*

That Sunday, an usher handed me a note: *"The deaf lady from Walmart is here."* I stopped the service and brought her forward. I laid hands on her ears—nothing much happened. A little hearing, but not much. I prayed again. Better, but still not whole. So I told her, *"I'm going to continue preaching. When your ears open fully, stand up and let me know."*

Fifteen minutes later she jumped up and shouted that she was hearing perfectly! The place erupted in praise. And yes, I still gave her the $100.

That's why Jesus could go into the wilderness and draw crowds by the thousands. He wasn't begging people with programs and giveaways. Signs and wonders drew them.

I'm not against feeding or clothing people—we should. But if the Church becomes only a social service organization, we've missed it. We're called to be a miracle organization. That's what's normal for the new creation.

And how does it happen? Not because of anything you've done, but because of who He is and what He's made you to be.

So this year, change the way you think. Change the way you see yourself. Start seeing yourself as Christ.

When you do, you'll walk taller. Your head will be up, your back straight, maybe even a little bounce in your step. Why? Because you know who you are: a new creation in Christ.

And when you know who you are, what Satan throws at you just falls off.

How can something that's already been defeated defeat you—unless you don't realize it's been defeated?

NINE
WHAT'S POSSIBLE

Is it possible that we've watered down this life so much that we're not accessing what's actually available to us?

Think about it. If I can look at Moses, Joshua, Elijah, and Elisha—sinners under the Old Covenant—and be amazed at what they did, then what does that say about the possibilities for a Christian who is united with Christ and seated at the right hand of God? That's the *lowest level* glimpse of what's available to us.

This is the question I've been asking myself for years now: *What's possible?*

It's the whisper I hear all the time: *What's possible? What's possible for a man or woman filled with God? What's possible for someone united with Him? What's possible for the one made perfect and complete in Him?*

You might say, *"Oh, you don't know what I've done."* No, you don't understand what Jesus did.

What's possible for someone where sin is no longer the issue, where sin is no longer the dominating factor? If you've still got sin clinging to your life, it's only because you don't know who you are. The moment you understand who you are, it falls off. Why? Because you'll start walking in your true identity.

That's why Paul said, *"As you received Him, so walk in Him."* (Colossians 2:6)

It's in Him I live. It's in Him I move. It's in Him I have my being. (Acts 17:28)

I am bone of His bone and flesh of His flesh. (Ephesians 5:30)

So if you're having bone or joint issues—remember, you're bone of His bone. If you're having skin issues—you're flesh of His flesh. No matter the physical issue, you're a branch connected to the Vine. His life flows in you.

We've all heard the phrase, *"You might be the only Jesus someone ever sees."* Usually, that's said in reference to your behavior—don't sin, act right. But what if we flip it?

What if you're the only Jesus someone with cancer ever

encounters? What if you're the only carrier of God a sinner meets?

What's the possibility that you really are the fullness of Him who fills all in all? What's the possibility that when you walk into a room, you're carrying Him in full, overflowing measure?

Don't water it down with clichés. Don't say, *"We're the hands and feet of Jesus,"* but then deny the results of Jesus.

Remember WWJD—What Would Jesus Do? We turned it into a slogan about behavior. But let's take it up a notch.

What would Jesus do with paralysis?

What would Jesus do with blindness?

What would Jesus do with cancer?

What would Jesus do with a virus?

That's the standard.

We've got to elevate our thinking. Expand our soul so we can expand our dominion. The world is crying out for the sons of God to rise up and say, *"Here we are!"* But sadly, much of the Church is still crying out for God to do something—blind to the fact that God already filled them with Himself so *they* could do something.

So I want to encourage you right now: it's time to advance. It's time to recognize that when you were born again, you were placed in Him, and He was placed in you.

Your identity is no longer tied to your skin color, your last name, your zip code, or your area code. Your identity is Him.

When I got born again, I got married into Him. I took His name. I took His identity. I took His bank account. I took His disease-prevention plan. He became my Husband and Provider. He became my Head, and I became His responsibility.

So why would I turn back to the world I was delivered from to deliver me?

> **Galatians 2:20 TPT**
>
> *My old identity has been co-crucified with Christ and no longer lives. And now the essence of this new life is no longer mine, for the Anointed One lives His life through me —we live in union as one! My new life is empowered by the faith of the Son of God who loves me so much that He gave Himself for me, and dispenses His life into mine!*

This is the reality: It's Christ who lives in me. The Anointed One and His anointing. The One with all glory, all power, all authority in heaven and on earth—that One lives in me, breathes in me, ministers through me, lays hands on the sick through me.

It's the Christ inside of me!

ABOUT THE AUTHOR

Dr. Chad Gonzales is the founder of *The Healing Academy*, host of *The Way Of Life* television program and *The Supernatural Life Podcast.* He holds a Master of Education and Doctorate of Ministry. Throughout the US and internationally, Chad has helped thousands experience miraculous healings; he is on a global mission to help the everyday believer walk according to the standard of Jesus Christ Himself.

OTHER BOOKS WRITTEN BY CHAD

Advance

Advance: The Devotional

Aliens

An Alternate Reality

Believing God For A House

Eight Percent

Fearless

God's Will Is You Healed

Jesus Is the Standard

Making Right Decisions

Naturally Supernatural

Never Be Sick Again

The Freedom of Forgiveness

The God Adventures of Riley & Rocky

The Supernatural Prayer of Jesus

Think Like Jesus

Walking In The Miraculous

PRAYER FOR SALVATION AND THE BAPTISM OF THE HOLY SPIRIT

Dear friend, it is the desire of God that everyone accepts His free gift of salvation. God sent the greatest gift Heaven had so the world could be set free; that precious gift was Jesus! Despite knowing the mistakes you would make, He died for you anyway. Jesus knew the mistakes you would make, yet He still climbed up on the cross. Why? His love was greater than your sin.

Romans 10:9-10 says if you will confess Jesus as your Lord and Savior and believe that He arose from the dead, you will be saved. You see, salvation has nothing to do with works. It doesn't matter what church you belong to, how many little old ladies you help across the street or how much you give the church. You cannot earn salvation; you cannot buy salvation; you must simply accept salvation.

Another free gift that God has provided is the Baptism of the Holy Spirit. In Acts 2, we find the Baptism of the Holy Spirit being given to the Church. God desires that you be filled with His Spirit with the evidence of speaking in tongues.

God said in Acts 2:38 that this life changing gift was for everyone, not just a select few. It wasn't just for those living in Bible days; it was given to everyone who would accept Jesus as Lord and Savior. Jesus said the purpose of the Baptism of the Holy Spirit was so you could be a witness! You'll find that when you receive the Baptism of the Holy Spirit, it allows you to operate in the fullness of God's power and be a blessing to the entire world. Essentially, you could say that salvation gets you into a relationship with God and the Baptism of the Holy Spirit helps you get others into a relationship with God.

Regardless of who you are, God has a plan for your life. He wants you to be successful, have all your needs met and live a life of victory. God wants every day of your life to be a day full of peace and joy, but it all begins with Jesus being your Lord and Savior. If you have never accepted Jesus as your Lord and Savior, please pray this prayer with me right now:

Jesus, I confess that I am a sinner. I realize I can't do this on my own. I believe with my heart and confess with my mouth that you died on the cross for my sins and sicknesses and arose from the dead. I ask you to be the Lord and Savior of my life. I thank you for forgiving me of my sins and loving me enough to give your life for me. I thank you that I am now a child of God! I now ask you for the Baptism of the Holy Spirit. You said in Your Word that it was a free gift so I receive it now. I thank you for my Heavenly prayer language!

We encourage you to become involved in a solid Bible based church. If you need help finding a church in your area, contact us through the information below.

Begin reading your Bible and praying in the Spirit daily. Now it is time to start developing your relationship with your Heavenly Father and growing in the Lord - and don't forget to tell someone about what Jesus did for you! Remember that God is good and He has good things in store for you!

If you prayed this prayer, would like assistance in locating a local church or this book has impacted your life, we would love to hear from you! You can also obtain a full listing of our books and other teaching materials by contacting us at: **www.ChadGonzales.com**

56   PRAYER FOR SALVATION AND THE BAPTISM OF T...

THE SUPERNATURAL LIFE PODCAST

Check out *The Supernatural Life Podcast* with Chad Gonzales! New episodes are available each month designed to help you connect with God on a deeper level and live the supernatural life God desires for you to have.

THE HEALING ACADEMY

The Healing Academy is an outreach of Chad Gonzales Ministries to help the everyday believer learn to walk according to the standard of Jesus in the ministry of healing.

Jesus said in John 14:12 that whoever believes in Him would do the same works and even greater works. Through *The Healing Academy*, it is our goal to raise the standard of the healing ministry in the Church and manifest the ministry of Jesus in the marketplace.

The Healing Academy is available online as well as in person training. For more information, please visit thehealingacademy.com

MORE FROM CGM

Looking to attend a live event with Chad? Visit chadgonzales.com/schedule or scan the QR code to find an event near you.

www.ingramcontent.com/pod-product-compliance
Lightning Source LLC
Chambersburg PA
CBHW060427050426
42449CB00009B/2181